Health and *Safety*

Joanne Suter

and

Susan M. Freese

LIFESKILLS HANDBOOKS

21st CENTURY

SADDLEBACK
EDUCATIONAL PUBLISHING

ISBN-13: 978-1-61651-657-4
ISBN-10: 1-61651-657-7
eBook: 978-1-61247-345-1

Printed in Guangzhou, China
1111/CA21101811

16 15 14 13 12   1 2 3 4 5

Contents

Prevention:
The Best Cure

Good health is something many people take for granted. But then something happens, and they're not healthy anymore. You can protect your health by developing healthy habits. Learn about the importance of regular exercise, good hygiene, and proper nutrition. And learn how to prevent accidents and be safe at home.

Making Good Health a Habit

Hector hated walking with crutches. Thankfully, he wouldn't have to use them for long. He had only sprained his ankle, not broken it.

Hector also hated telling people how he'd gotten hurt. He had fallen at home!

Hector and his family had known for months that the carpet on the stairs was loose. They'd talked about fixing it every time one of them slipped and came close to falling. Tacking down the loose carpet would have been a simple repair and taken only a few minutes. But for some reason, it had never been done.

Telling people he had fallen was embarrassing for Hector. After all, he was an athlete. He'd been hurt a couple of times playing soccer but not seriously. He had always been in good shape, so he'd recovered from those injuries pretty quickly. Even in the offseason, he kept himself physically fit. He ran and worked out at the gym year round.

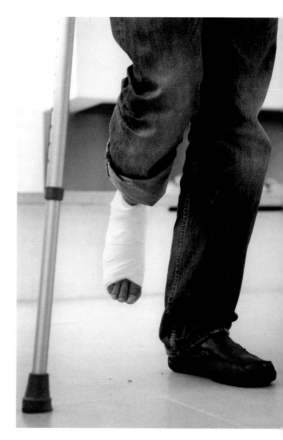

Hector ate well year round, too. It wasn't always easy. He was busy with his job and school and working out. A lot of his friends ate foods that were

quick and easy to get. They went to fast-food restaurants and bought snacks from vending machines. But Hector knew that if he didn't eat well, he wouldn't feel well. And if he didn't feel well, he wouldn't get things done.

Hector also did everything he could to avoid catching a cold or the flu. Living in a house with five other people made that a challenge. His mother reminded everyone to wash their hands and to develop other habits to prevent the spread of germs. She teased Hector about "not having time to get sick."

Hector knew one thing he would make time for: fixing the carpet on the stairs.

CHAPTER **1**

Physical Fitness

Think about the challenges your body faced today. Did you run to the bus stop? Did you carry a heavy backpack? Did you play a sport?

Your body's ability to meet these daily demands is called *physical fitness*. Regular exercise is one of the keys to physical fitness. It helps you stay healthy and look and feel your best.

Aerobic Exercise

Aerobic exercise strengthens your heart. During aerobic exercise, you breathe in more oxygen (air), and your body uses it in an effective way. Aerobic exercise makes your heart beat faster. It pumps more blood

to your muscles and provides them with more oxygen. Aerobic power helps you do hard, physical work.

> **Aerobic**
> Using or related to the body's use of oxygen.

Swimming, biking, walking, and running are examples of aerobic exercise. Lifting weights is an example of muscle-building or strength-training exercise. It is not an aerobic activity.

How much aerobic exercise is enough? The Mayo Clinic says to do at least 30 minutes of aerobic activity a day. Getting regular exercise can help you live a longer and healthier life.

Walking as Aerobic Exercise

- **Leisure walking:** Stroll at a light to moderate pace.
- **Race walking or power walking:** This form of walking comes close to running. To do it, pick up your pace and pump your arms.
- **Hill walking:** After walking on flat ground at a moderate pace for 5 to 10 minutes, walk up a hill at a steady pace. Then walk down the hill and back up again.
- **Interval training:** Start with a warm-up by walking at a light pace for 5 to 10 minutes. Next, walk as quickly as you can for 20 seconds. Then walk at a normal pace for 40 to 60 seconds. Continue to switch back and forth between a fast and a normal speed.

No More Excuses!

Many people make excuses for not exercising. But there's a way to argue against every common excuse:

- **"I don't have enough time to exercise."** Fit exercise into your regular activities:

  —Walk 5 to 10 minutes throughout the entire day, not all at once.

  —Drive less and walk more. Park your car at the far edge of the parking lot.

  —Replace some kind of weekly entertainment with a physical activity. For instance, instead of going to a movie with friends, go bike riding.

- **"Exercise is boring."** Find something you enjoy doing—anything that gets you moving.

- **"I'm worried how I'll look at the gym."** Exercise alone at home with a DVD or game system video. Think about how you'll improve and look better over time.

- **"I'm too tired when I get home from work."** Bring your workout gear with you so you don't go home after work, or have your gear ready to go when you walk in the door. Also try exercising earlier in the day.

- **"I'm too lazy!"** Exercise at the time of day you feel most energetic. Plan a schedule and stick to it. Start with a short walk. Ask others to support you.

Guidelines for Stretching

- Don't stretch your muscles when they're cold. Walk at a light pace for 5 or 10 minutes before doing your warm-up stretch. Then stretch again after you exercise.
- Stretch all of your major muscle groups, not just your legs. Also, be sure to stretch both sides of your body.
- Don't bounce when you stretch. Instead, hold the stretch for approximately 30 seconds. Repeat each stretch three or four times.
- Don't stretch to the point that you hurt. You should feel tension, not pain.
- Add movement to your stretching. For instance, reach up or out with your arms while stretching your legs. Think of the movements used in yoga and the martial arts.

Play It Safe!

Exercise is a *must* for good health, but be sure to exercise safely. Warm up first to loosen your muscles before you put them to work. And stretch before exercising to reduce the chance of injury.

After your activity, make sure to give your muscles time to cool down and relax.

Benefits of Exercise

Most people who exercise regularly say they couldn't get along without it! Scientists have found that the body releases special chemicals during exercise. Those chemicals, called *endorphins*, create a sense of

well-being and reduce feelings of stress.

Exercise has other benefits, too. It helps you maintain your proper weight by burning *calories*. The following chart shows how much exercise you have to do to burn off the calories in a couple of popular foods. The numbers in the chart are for someone who weighs 150 pounds.

> **Calorie**
>
> A unit measuring how much energy is used.

Burning Off the Calories

This Food . . .	Has This Many Calories . . .	Takes This Much Exercise to Burn Off . . .		
		Minutes of Walking (4 miles per hour)	Minutes of High-Impact Aerobics	Minutes of Running (5.2 miles per hour)
Quarter-pound cheeseburger with bun	552	103	66	51
Chocolate chip muffin	364	67	44	34
One slice of pizza, meat and veggies, thick crust	233	43	28	22

People use calories at different rates, depending on how much they weigh. If you weigh 75 pounds, you will use half as many calories as a 150-pound person doing the same exercise for the same amount of time.

Figure out how many calories you burn doing different activities by using the "Calorie Calculator" at this Web site: www.healthdiscovery .net/links/calculators/calorie_calculator.htm.

And find out how many calories are in your favorite foods at MyFood-a-pedia: www.myfoodapedia.gov. This Web site is maintained by the US Department of Agriculture (USDA).

[FACT]

Calories Burned Per Hour by Different Activities

Activity (1 hour)	Calories Burned by Someone Weighing (in pounds):				
	130	155	180	205	240
Aerobics (low impact)	295	352	409	465	545
Ballroom dancing (slow)	177	211	245	279	327
Basketball game (competitive)	472	563	654	745	872
Bicycling (less than 10 miles per hour)	236	281	327	372	436
Football (flag or touch)	472	563	654	745	872
Hiking (cross-country)	354	422	490	558	654
Ice skating (average speed)	413	493	572	651	763
Martial arts	590	704	817	931	1,090
Rollerblading/Inline skating	708	844	981	1117	1,363
Rowing machine (moderate pace)	413	493	572	651	763
Running (5 miles per hour)	472	563	654	745	872
Skiing (cross-country)	413	493	572	651	763
Softball or baseball	295	352	409	465	545
Swimming laps (slow)	413	493	572	651	763
Walking slowly (2 miles per hour)	148	176	204	233	273
Walking quickly (3.5 miles per hour)	224	267	311	354	414
Weightlifting (light workout)	177	211	245	279	327

CHAPTER **2**

Hygiene

People look better and feel better when they're clean. Good *hygiene* habits can put you on the road to good health and help protect you from germs.

Hygiene

Habits related to being clean and maintaining good health.

How Good Is Your Hygiene?

Check your hygiene by answering the following questions:

Guarding against Germs

Do you . . .

Yes   No

☐ ☐ 1. Shower or bathe regularly?

☐ ☐ 2. Wash your hands often with soap and water?

☐ ☐ 3. Wash the fronts and backs of your hands and between your fingers and thumbs?

☐ ☐ 4. Wash your hands long enough? (You should be able to sing the "Happy Birthday" song twice.)

☐ ☐ 5. Dry your hands with a clean towel after washing?

☐ ☐ 6. Cover your nose with a tissue when you sneeze or sneeze into your upper sleeve?

☐ ☐ 7. Cover your mouth with a tissue or the back of your hand when you cough?

Having Healthy Hair

Do you . . .

Yes   No

☐ ☐ 1. Wash your hair regularly?

☐ ☐ 2. Use an anti-dandruff shampoo if you have a flaky scalp?

☐ ☐ 3. Follow the directions on the shampoo bottle?

☐ ☐ 4. Regularly clean your combs, brushes, and pillowcases?

☐ ☐ 5. Wear only your own hats and use only your own combs and brushes?

Using Hand Sanitizers

Washing your hands is a good way to get rid of germs. But should you use soap and water or a gel or liquid hand sanitizer?

Not everyone agrees on which is best. Here are the benefits and drawbacks of using hand sanitizers:

Benefits

- Sanitizers with at least 60% alcohol can kill most bacteria (germs).
- A small bottle of sanitizer is easy to carry with you.
- You can use a sanitizer when soap and water aren't available.

Drawbacks

- Sanitizers don't kill viruses, including those that cause colds.
- Sanitizers don't wash away dirt. You need soap and water for that.
- Sanitizers kill both good and bad bacteria. Good bacteria help you stay healthy.
- Sanitizers are flammable (will start on fire).
- Sanitizers are poisonous if swallowed.

Taking Care of Your Teeth

Do you . . .

Yes   No

☐ ☐ 1. Brush your teeth every morning and night and after eating?

☐ ☐ 2. Brush both the outside and inside surfaces of your teeth?

☐ ☐ 3. Brush your tongue to remove germs that can cause bad breath?

Avoiding Germs in Public Restrooms

- Flush the toilet by pressing the handle with your foot, not your hand.
- Wash your hands thoroughly with soap and warm water.
- Use a clean paper towel to turn off the faucet after you've washed your hands.
- Try not to touch the surface of a hot-air hand dryer.
- Use your forearm or elbow to push the button or lever to get a paper towel.
- Don't set your belongings on the counter or floor.
- When you're ready to leave, use a paper towel to open the door.

Yes   No

☐   ☐   4. Rinse your mouth well with water or mouthwash after brushing?

☐   ☐   5. Floss your teeth at least once a day?

☐   ☐   6. Have regular dental check-ups?

☐   ☐   7. Eat a well-balanced diet?

☐   ☐   8. Avoid sugary foods and drinks?

Taking Care of Your Skin

Do you . . .

Yes   No

☐   ☐   1. Drink plenty of water (at least eight glasses a day)?

☐   ☐   2. Wash your face at least twice a day (morning and night)?

☐   ☐   3. Wash your face after physical workouts?

Yes   No

☐   ☐   4. Know your skin type (dry, oily, or combination) and use skin products that are right for you?

☐   ☐   5. Keep your hair clean and off your face?

☐   ☐   6. Avoid squeezing pimples, blackheads, and whiteheads?

☐   ☐   7. See a ***dermatologist*** about severe skin problems?

How Did You Do?

How many questions did you answer "Yes"? Your "Yes" answers point out your good hygiene habits.

Dermatologist

A doctor who specializes in treating the skin.

How many questions did you answer "No"? Your "No" answers point out areas of hygiene that you need to work on.

What's Wrong with Sharing?

Sharing items such as combs, brushes, hats, and pillows can cause health problems. Sharing can spread tiny insects called *head lice*. Lice nest and lay eggs in the hair. They make the scalp itch, and scratching can lead to sores and infection. Lice can even cause the hair to fall out.

Getting rid of lice can be hard. You need to wash your hair with shampoo that contains a medicine. You also need to wash combs, brushes, and even bedding. You may need to throw away items such as hats and scarves.

To prevent lice, don't share items that touch the hair. And avoid close contact with someone who has lice.

Acne

Acne is a skin condition that usually appears on the face, shoulders, and back. It's commonly called *pimples* or *zits*. Acne occurs when your pores—those tiny holes on the surface of your skin—become clogged with oil, dirt, and bacteria. This causes whiteheads, blackheads, and swollen, red bumps to form. The bumps are sometimes called *blemishes*.

How can you treat acne?

1. **Start with self-care.**

   - Wash your skin once or twice a day (including after exercise) with mild soap.

   - Shampoo your hair every day, if it's oily. And keep your hair away from your face.

   - Avoid sugary and starchy foods, such as white bread, white rice, pasta, and potatoes.

   - Don't squeeze, scratch, pick, or rub blackheads, whiteheads, or pimples.

   - Don't wear headbands or hats that touch your forehead or the sides of your face.

   - Avoid touching your face.

   - Avoid wearing oily makeup, and remove makeup at night.

2. **Next, try the drugstore.** Ask the pharmacist to suggest an over-the-counter acne medicine.

3. **Finally, see your doctor.** If you're still having problems, see your doctor and ask about a prescription medicine.

CHAPTER 3

Nutrition

Eating nutritious foods is another important step you can take to keep yourself healthy. Eating a nutritious diet can help you feel fit and look good.

What's on Your Plate?

What is a nutritious diet? What kinds of foods should you eat? And in what amounts?

The US Department of Agriculture (USDA) has developed guidelines for a nutritious diet. Look at the illustration below, which is from the USDA's Web site: www.ChooseMyPlate.gov. This "plate" shows the **categories** of foods you should eat every day and in what general amounts.

Categories

Types or groups.

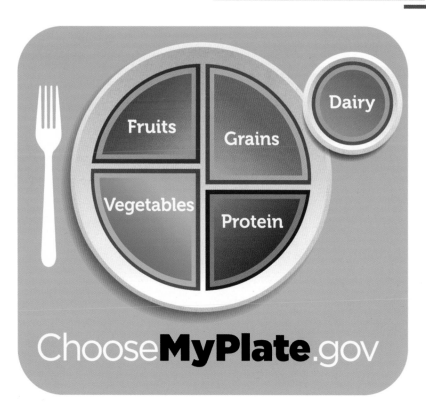

Make Good Choices

To help you choose foods from these five categories, the USDA offers these guidelines:

1. **Grains: "Make at least half your grains whole."**
   Whole grains include oats, brown rice, bulgur, barley, and rye. White breads, rices, and flours have fewer health benefits.

2. **Vegetables: "Vary your veggies."**
   Choose a mix of colors of vegetables: green, red, orange, and yellow. Different-colored vegetables have different health benefits.

3. **Fruits: "Focus on fruits."**
   Eat fresh fruit as much as possible, rather than canned or frozen. And drink 100% fruit juice, not sugar-flavored fruit drinks.

4. **Dairy: "Get your calcium-rich foods."**
   Calcium is important for building strong bones. Switch to fat-free or low-fat dairy products.

5. **Protein: "Go lean with protein."**
   Meat is a good source of protein. But look for lean, low-fat cuts of meat. Beans and nuts are also good sources of protein.

[FACT]

New USDA Food Guidelines

The US Department of Agriculture (USDA) has provided guidelines for nutritious eating for many years. In 2010, the model for those guidelines changed from a "pyramid" to a "plate." The basic categories of foods stayed the same, but the recommended amounts changed.

What was the main reason for the change? Too many Americans are overweight. According to some estimates, one in three Americans is *obese*, or seriously overweight. And almost one in five children are obese.

To control your weight, the USDA makes two simple suggestions:

1. Eat less.   2. Move more.

The USDA also **recommends** eating more of and less of certain foods:

Eat More of These Foods

→ Fruits and vegetables

→ Whole-grain breads and other grains

→ Fat-free or low-fat milk

→ Water

Eat Less of These Foods

→ Canned, boxed, and frozen foods

→ Sugary drinks, such as soda and fruit-based beverages

Recommend
To suggest something is a good idea.

Know What You're Eating

Another government agency, the US Food and Drug Administration (FDA), requires that food companies live up to the *claims* they make about their products. To be sure of what you're eating, look for these terms on product labels:

→ **"Free," as in "sugar-free":** The product contains none or almost none of the ingredient.

→ **"Fresh," as in "fresh grapefruit juice":** The product is raw and has not been heated or frozen.

→ **"High," as in "high in fiber":** The product provides 20% or more of the daily value (DV) of the *nutrient* per serving.

→ **"Light" or "Lite," as in "lite cream cheese":** The product's label must say how it's different from the normal or original food. For example, it may contain one-third fewer calories or one-half the fat or sodium of the regular product.

→ **"A good source of," as in "a good source of calcium":** A serving of the product provides 10% to 19% percent of the DV of the nutrient named.

Claims

Things that are said to be true.

Nutrients

Nutritious substances, such as calcium and protein.

Tips for Healthy Snacks

- **Enjoy fresh fruits and vegetables.** Buy snack-ready fruits and veggies, such as grapes and baby carrots, or cut up your own. Keep containers of washed and cut-up veggie sticks in the refrigerator. And keep bowls of apples, pears, and bananas on the kitchen table or counter.

- **Carry dried fruit.** Dried fruit comes in many varieties, and it's lightweight and long lasting.

- **Think protein.** Peanut butter, hummus, and yogurt are good dips for fruit and veggies. Cheese, milk, and nuts also are good sources of protein.

- **Choose whole grains.** When choosing crackers and breads, look for whole-grain products. Also snack on rice cakes, mini-bagels, graham crackers, and popcorn (with little or no salt and butter).

- **Make cold treats.** Make "juice pops" by freezing 100% juice in small cups. Or make a "smoothie" by blending fruit and yogurt.

- **Bake your own treats.** Add whole-grain flour or oats to cookies. Reduce the amount of sugar in recipes.

CHAPTER 4

Staying Safe at Home

What's the first thing you should buy to make your home safe? A high-tech security system? Some sturdy dead-bolt locks? A fire extinguisher?

You'll probably be surprised to know that the answer is something quite simple: a rubber bath mat! More people are injured in the bathtub than any other part of the house. Having a rubber bath mat will help prevent slips and falls.

So, here's home safety rule number 1: *Use a rubber bath mat.*

In fact, most home accidents take place in the bathroom, in the kitchen, or on the stairs. Learning some basic safety rules for these common areas will help you prevent accidents at home.

Jake and Jen's Home Safety Tour

Jake and Jen really need some help with home safety! Think about how many of the same safety issues exist at your house, too.

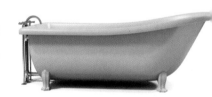

Problem #1: The Bathroom

Jake has had a long day and wants to take a bath. He's decided to listen to some tunes at the same time. He plugs in his radio next to the bathtub and hops right in. But he can't hear the music over the sound of the running water. So, he reaches out to turn up the sound and . . .

Can you see the problems in this situation? Jake needs to learn several safety rules for the bathroom:

→ Never use a hairdryer, radio (except a shower radio), TV, or other electrical device near water. And don't touch any electrical device when you're wet. Electricity and water don't mix. You might get **electrocuted**.

→ Check the temperature of the water before you get into the tub. You can get burned if the water is too hot.

Here are some more rules for bathroom safety:

→ Keep cleaning supplies and medicines in a cupboard or closet out of children's reach.

→ Use **childproof** caps on pill bottles.

→ Throw away pills that are old or are no longer being used.

→ Keep floors clean and dry to prevent slipping.

Problem #2: The Kitchen

Jen is busy cooking. She has a pot on the stove with the handle facing out, toward her. Then, she spills a cup of milk on the floor. She leaves it for the cat to lap up later. Next, Jen takes raw meat off the cutting board and puts it in a pan. Then she put a pear on the same cutting board and starts to slice it up.

Electrocuted
Being injured or killed by an electric shock.

Childproof
Something that has been made safe for children. Also the act of making something safe for children.

Jen's kitchen is full of safety hazards! She needs to learn and follow these rules:

→ Turn the handles of all pots toward the back of the stove and away from other burners. Never point them toward the front. It's too easy to knock a pot off the stove and spill the hot contents onto you. Also, pointing handles toward other burners will make the handles hot and you'll get burned.

Preventing Cross-Contamination

Cross-contamination happens when bacteria (or germs) from one food are passed to another food. This can happen easily when foods are stored, cut, or prepared on the same surfaces or using the same containers. And the result can be food poisoning.

Follow these tips to avoid cross-contamination:

- **Shopping and storing foods in the refrigerator:** Put packages of raw meat in plastic bags to keep the juices from dripping onto other foods. Refrigerate raw eggs immediately.

- **Preparing foods:** Wash hands, kitchen surfaces, utensils, and cutting boards often with hot, soapy water. Wash fruits and vegetables before eating or preparing them, and remove the outer leaves on heads of lettuce and cabbage. If soaking meat in a marinade (sauce), keep it in the refrigerator. Throw out or boil the leftover marinade before using it on cooked food.

- **Serving foods:** Place all foods on clean plates or in clean bowls. Never put cooked foods on a plate that has held raw meat.

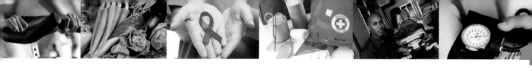

→ **Don't** wait to wipe up spills. Someone might slip on them.

→ Raw meat can carry germs. Thoroughly clean anything that raw meat touches before putting it away or using it for something else.

Here are some more kitchen hints:

→ **Don't** use water on a grease fire. Instead, dump baking soda on the flames. To be extra safe, keep a fire extinguisher nearby, and make sure that it's in working order.

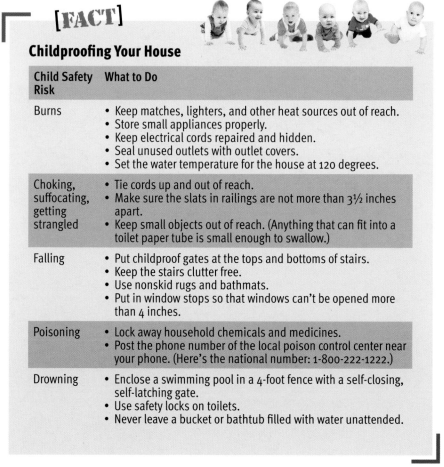

[FACT]

Childproofing Your House

Child Safety Risk	What to Do
Burns	• Keep matches, lighters, and other heat sources out of reach. • Store small appliances properly. • Keep electrical cords repaired and hidden. • Seal unused outlets with outlet covers. • Set the water temperature for the house at 120 degrees.
Choking, suffocating, getting strangled	• Tie cords up and out of reach. • Make sure the slats in railings are not more than 3½ inches apart. • Keep small objects out of reach. (Anything that can fit into a toilet paper tube is small enough to swallow.)
Falling	• Put childproof gates at the tops and bottoms of stairs. • Keep the stairs clutter free. • Use nonskid rugs and bathmats. • Put in window stops so that windows can't be opened more than 4 inches.
Poisoning	• Lock away household chemicals and medicines. • Post the phone number of the local poison control center near your phone. (Here's the national number: 1-800-222-1222.)
Drowning	• Enclose a swimming pool in a 4-foot fence with a self-closing, self-latching gate. • Use safety locks on toilets. • Never leave a bucket or bathtub filled with water unattended.

- → To unplug an electrical kitchen device, pull the plug out of the socket. Never pull on the cord.

- → Childproof all cupboards. The kitchen is full of utensils and cleaners that are dangerous to children and pets.

- → Refrigerate foods that come in bottles and jars after opening them. And don't keep leftovers in the refrigerator for more than a few days.

[FACT]

Preventing Fires at Home

Top Causes of Fires	Safety Tips
1. Cooking equipment	• Keep appliances clean and dry. • Don't wear scarves or clothes with loose sleeves when cooking at the stove. • Keep potholders, dishtowels, and curtains 3 feet from the stove. • For a microwave or oven fire, keep the door of the appliance closed. Then turn off heat. • For a grease fire, slide a cover over the pan. Then turn off heat.
2. Heating equipment	• Never leave a space heater running when leaving the room. • Use a space heater that will shut off by itself if it overheats. • Keep heating equipment 3 feet from anything that can burn. • Don't use an extension cord to plug in a heater. Plug it directly into an outlet.
3. Electrical equipment	• Fix or replace frayed or loose cords on appliances. • Avoid using extension cords. • Don't run cords under rugs or carpet. • Don't overload electrical outlets by plugging in too many appliances.
4. Smoking	• Never smoke in bed. • Before going to bed, look for burning cigarettes in trashcans and under cushions. • Check the carpet around ashtrays.

[FACT]

Top-Five Home Injuries

1. **Falling**
   - Tripping on rugs, electric cords, and cluttered stairs
   - Slipping on a wet floor or in the bathtub
   - Falling from a ladder

2. **Poisoning**
   - Taking a dangerous mixture of substances, such as prescription drugs or a decongestant with an alcoholic drink
   - Misusing a medicine or household chemical that's not labeled correctly

3. **Burns and electrocution**
   - Getting into hot bathwater or spilling a hot drink
   - Getting burned from cigarettes, matches, or a faulty appliance
   - Getting electrocuted from using an appliance near water

4. **Suffocation and choking**
   - Choking on food or a small object
   - Being smothered by a plastic bag or by extra pillows or toys in bed
   - Getting tangled in cords, strings, or necklaces

5. **Drowning**
   - Falling so that the head goes into the toilet or a bucket of water
   - Drowning in a bathtub, hot tub, or pool

SECTION **2**

Getting Medical Attention

Being unhealthy isn't just frustrating. It's also expensive. That's why it's important to have health insurance. Knowing that your doctors' visits will be paid for makes it more likely that you'll get medical care on a regular basis. Your regular medical care should also include visits to the dentist. And if you're struggling with an emotional problem, you should get the help of a mental health professional.

Getting the Help You Need

Audrey was having a tough time. Six months ago, she'd lost her full-time job when the company she worked for laid off 20 employees.

Since then, Audrey had held two part-time jobs. She was managing to pay her rent and other expenses. But she'd had to cut back on going out with her friends. She seemed to be home a lot. And she seemed to be alone a lot, too.

Audrey didn't want to complain. She knew other people who were worse off than she was. But she felt like everything was going wrong.

First, she lost her job. Then three weeks later, she got in a car accident. It wasn't serious, thankfully. Her car had hardly any damage, and she didn't think she was hurt. But soon, her neck and back started to ache.

Audrey thought about going to the doctor. But because she'd

lost her job, she didn't have health insurance anymore. She knew that getting medical attention would be expensive. She couldn't afford to pay more bills, so she didn't go.

A month or so after the accident, Audrey chipped a tooth. She wanted to go to the dentist, but she didn't have dental insurance anymore, either. The tooth didn't hurt much, but she hated how it looked and felt. She would just have to live with it, she decided.

Several weeks later, Audrey and her boyfriend broke up. Things between them had been tense since Audrey had lost her job. "You're so moody!" he finally told her. She had to admit that she wasn't much fun to be around.

Audrey's mother told her that things would get better. "You're just feeling blue," she said. But Audrey wasn't so sure. Things seemed pretty hopeless.

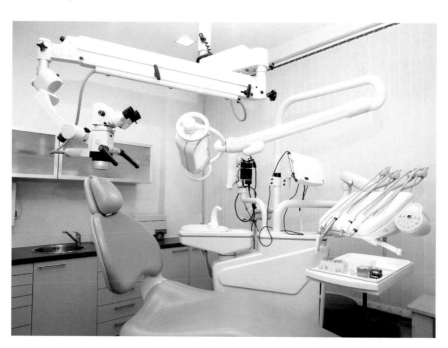

CHAPTER 1

Health Insurance

Health insurance helps people afford getting medical treatment. It pays for some health care costs, such as doctor visits, hospital stays, surgeries, and laboratory tests. Some health insurance pays for prescription medicines and devices such as glasses and hearing aids.

Terms to Know

To understand kinds of health insurance and how they work, you need to know the following terms:

Benefit: The amount of money paid to a medical *provider*.

Claim: A request for payment under the terms of a health insurance *policy*.

Provider

An individual or group that delivers health care, such as a doctor or clinic.

Policy

The contract or agreement that outlines the terms of insurance coverage.

Co-pay: A set amount of money (usually small) that someone with insurance pays for drugs or services such as doctors' visits.

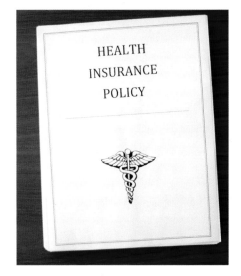

Coverage: The type of insurance someone has and the level of care that will be paid for.

Deductible: The amount of money that someone with insurance must pay each year before the insurance company begins to pay for medical care.

Exclusion: A *condition* or treatment that the insurance company won't pay for.

HMO (Health Maintenance Organization): A group health care plan that requires that care be managed by one doctor; that doctor is chosen from a list of approved providers.

Pre-existing condition: A condition someone had *before* applying for insurance; there is sometimes a waiting period before treatment for such a condition will be covered.

Premium: The monthly or yearly amount of money paid to have insurance coverage.

Primary care physician (PCP): Someone's main doctor.

Condition
A health problem or illness.

Types of Health Insurance

Two general types of health insurance are common today:

1. **Fee-for-services coverage:** This type of health insurance allows you to go to any health care provider you want to. But for this freedom of choice, you usually pay a higher premium.

2. **Managed care:** With this kind of health insurance, you select one provider to manage your care. Visits to other providers must be arranged by your primary care physician. Managed care costs less, but it limits your choice of doctors. And it may pay higher benefits to providers.

Who Needs Health Insurance?

Many young people don't think they need health insurance. They consider themselves healthy and not in need of health care. But anyone can get sick or have an accident, and everyone should have regular check-ups.

Most people can't afford the high costs of health care and couldn't get care if they didn't have health insurance. Study the following chart of what medical treatments cost in the United States. Ask yourself,

"Could I pay for that treatment out of my pocket?" If the answer is "no," then you need health insurance.

Medical Treatment	Sample Cost of Treatment
Stitches for a deep cut	$691
CT scan of head	$2,090
Appendectomy (surgery to remove infected appendix)	$15,850 (2-day hospital stay)

Tips for Getting Health Insurance

- **Get it before you need it.** Getting insurance is more difficult and will cost more after you've been injured or become sick.

- **Be honest on the application.** Don't lie about past medical conditions or treatments. The insurance company will find out about your medical history. Then later, it may use this information to cancel your policy or not cover your claim.

- **Buy only what you need, but protect yourself from debt.** If you're healthy, you may decide to have a policy with a high deductible. That way, you'll pay for all regular medical care, such as doctors' visits and prescriptions. 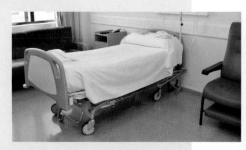 But you'll have coverage to pay for a serious accident or illness. Many people who have a bad accident or long-term illness end up deep in debt because they didn't have good health insurance.

- **Shop and compare.** Compare coverage and premiums at different health insurance companies. A good place to start is www.healthinsurance.org or http://finder.healthcare.gov.

Buying Your Own Health Insurance

- More than 26.5 million Americans are covered by health insurance plans they pay for themselves.

- The average amount they pay each year is $2,985 for a single person and $6,328 for a family.

- The cost varies greatly from state to state. For example, in New York, the average cost for a family is $13,296. But in Iowa, the same insurance plan costs $5,609.

HMO Benefits Summary

Network Benefits
Annual Deductible

Types of Coverage
This Benefit Summary is intended only to highlight your Benefits and should not be relied upon to fully determine coverage. This benefit plan may not cover all of your health care expenses. More complete descriptions of Benefits and the terms under which they are provided are contained in the Certificate of Coverage that you will receive upon enrolling in the Plan.

If this Benefit Summary conflicts in any way with the Contract issued to your employer, the Contract shall prevail.

Terms that are capitalized in the Benefit Summary are defined in the Certificate of Coverage.

Benefits are payable for Covered Health Services provided by or under the direction of your Network physician.

*Prior Notification is required for certain services.

1. Ambulance Services - Emergency only

2. Dental Services - Accident only

3. Durable Medical Equipment

4. Emergency Health Services

5. Eye Examinations

Where Do You Get Health Insurance?

Most people get health insurance through their work. Employers offer certain kinds of coverage and pay part or all of the premium. Having health insurance is an important employment **benefit**.

If you can't get health insurance through your work, you may need to buy an individual plan. Individual coverage is usually harder to get and more expensive than a group plan.

Benefits

The "extras" that an employer offers to employees, such as paid vacation, paid holidays, and health insurance.

[FACT]

Health Coverage through Your Parents

Are you under age 26? If so, and if your parents have health insurance, you can be added to their policy. The insurance company offers a 30-day period each year when new people can be added.

In 2010, the US government set this rule as part of the Affordable Care Act. You can be on your parents' plan whether or not you are any of the following:

- In school
- Living with your parents
- Financially dependent on your parents
- Married

CHAPTER 2

The Doctor's Office

Making an Appointment

Sarah has had an earache for five days. She knows that when a health problem won't go away, it's time to call the doctor.

Sarah calls Dr. Miller's office and talks to a nurse. Sarah explains that she's ill and would like to see the doctor. The nurse makes some notes about what Sarah tells her. And she gives Sarah a 3:00 p.m. appointment that day.

Sarah arrives at the office at 2:45. She'll use the 15 extra minutes to update her insurance information and fill out forms.

Routine Health Checks

A nurse takes Sarah to the examining room. The nurse makes several *routine* health checks before the doctor comes in. She weighs Sarah and checks her blood pressure, pulse rate, and temperature. She records the information on Sarah's chart.

Why are these routine health checks important? They're signs of overall health. For instance, blood pressure is the force of your blood against the walls of your arteries (blood vessels). It tells the doctor about the strength of your heart, the ease of your blood flow, and the health of your arteries. High blood pressure is a serious medical condition and can lead to other health problems.

Routine

Usual or normal. Done out of habit.

Temperature is another important health check. The body's normal temperature is 98.6 to 99.6 degrees Fahrenheit. A temperature that's higher than normal often indicates some kind of infection.

[FACT]

Understanding Blood Pressure Readings

As blood pumps from your heart to your arteries, the pressure of the blood against your artery walls changes. Routine checks of blood pressure measure the high and low levels of pressure:

1. **Systolic pressure** occurs when the heart beats. The pressure is usually highest at this point.

2. **Diastolic pressure** occurs when the heart rests between beats. The pressure is usually lowest at this point.

Blood pressure *readings*, or checks, report both types of pressure. A reading is like a fraction: The systolic pressure is on the top, and the diastolic pressure is on the bottom. For a blood pressure of 110/75, you would say "110 over 75."

Both numbers are important measures of heart health. Here's what they mean when combined in a blood pressure reading:

Systolic (Top) Number	Diastolic (Bottom) Number	Blood Pressure Condition	What to Do
Below 120	Below 80	Normal	Maintain or develop a healthy lifestyle.
120–139	80–89	Pre-hypertension	Maintain or develop a healthy lifestyle.
140–159	90–99	Stage 1 hypertension	Develop a healthier lifestyle. Set a blood pressure goal. If you don't reach it in 6 months, discuss medicine with your doctor.
160 or higher	100 or higher	Stage 2 hypertension (high blood pressure)	Develop a healthier lifestyle. Discuss adding more medicine with your doctor.

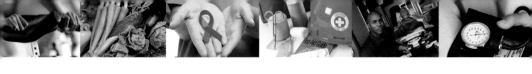

The Doctor's Examination

Alone in the examining room, Sarah checks her notes. She's come prepared to talk to the doctor.

Keeping a patient healthy isn't just the doctor's job. The patient has responsibilities, too. The doctor needs information from the patient to make the right *diagnosis* and to *prescribe* proper treatment. That information should include the following:

→ A list of problems or concerns

→ Allergies or *side effects* from medicines

→ Questions to ask the doctor

Diagnosis

The act or process of identifying an illness or disease.

Prescribe

To recommend a treatment, such as a medicine.

Side effects

The effects of taking a medicine that aren't related to the cure or treatment. Common side effects are having a headache and an upset stomach.

Soon, Dr. Miller comes in. She is a general practitioner. That means she works with the whole body and provides regular medical care. Sometimes, if a problem is very specific or severe, Dr. Miller sends a patient to a specialist. If Sarah's ear doesn't get better, Dr. Miller will make a ***referral*** to an ear, nose, and throat specialist.

First, Dr. Miller reviews Sarah's chart. Then, she conducts a complete examination. Next, a lab technician draws some blood. The lab tests show that Sarah has an ear infection, so Dr. Miller prescribes an antibiotic.

"We'll recheck your ear in 10 days," Dr. Miller says. "Please make an appointment on your way out."

Referral

A suggestion of someone to contact to provide a service.

[FACT]

Medical Specialists

- **Allergist:** allergic reactions, such as asthma and hay fever
- **Cardiologist:** heart and blood vessels
- **Dermatologist:** diseases of the skin
- **Endocrinologist:** hormone disorders, such as diabetes, bone diseases, and problems with metabolism (the body's process of turning food into energy)
- **Geriatrician:** conditions of the elderly
- **Gynecologist:** women's reproductive system
- **Hematologist:** blood disorders
- **Obstetrician:** pregnancy and childbirth
- **Oncologist:** cancer
- **Ophthalmologist:** diseases of the eye
- **Orthopedic surgeon:** injured or diseased bones and joints
- **Pediatrician:** babies and children
- **Psychiatrist:** mental illness

47

CHAPTER **3**

Dental Treatment

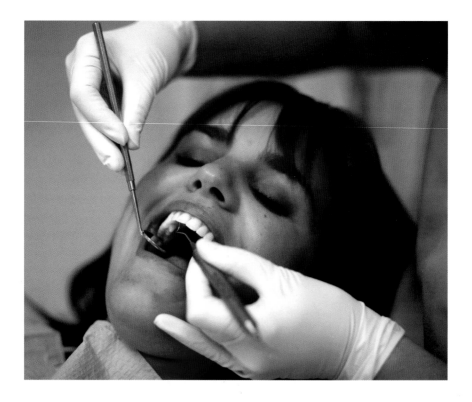

Bite! Chew! Talk! Smile! Your teeth get a big workout every day. You, your dentist, and the dental office staff make up the team that keeps your teeth and gums strong and healthy.

Most dental problems can be prevented with the proper care. But in some cases, other kinds of dental treatment are needed.

Preventive Care

The general recommendation is to have two dental check-ups a year. A regular visit will likely include the following:

→ Instructions on oral hygiene (tooth brushing and flossing)

→ Oral prophylaxis (routine teeth cleaning)

→ Treatments to prevent tooth decay (cavities), such as fluoride and tooth sealants (plastic materials bonded over grooves in the teeth)

→ An examination of the teeth and gums

→ X-rays to check for cavities, cracks, and other problems

Preventive
Done to avoid or protect.

[FACT]

Ten Common Dental Problems

Making regular visits to your dentist will help avoid or control these problems:

1. Bad breath
2. Gum disease
3. Mouth sores
4. Tooth sensitivity
5. Yellow teeth
6. Cavities
7. Wisdom teeth
8. Teeth grinding
9. Tooth erosion
10. Toothaches

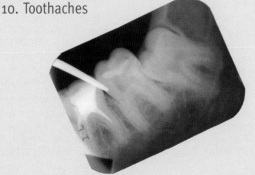

Emergency Care

Most dentists will see emergency cases right away. If your own dentist isn't available, the office can usually make a referral for emergency care.

What is a dental emergency?

→ Severe pain or bleeding

→ An injury to your teeth

Restorative Services

Dentists usually use fillings to repair the damage caused by tooth decay. Cavities may be filled with metal, porcelain, or gold.

Restorative
Done to renew or return to health or well-being.

Another kind of restorative service involves putting a crown over a tooth. A *crown* is an artificial tooth that fits over a real tooth. Crowns are sometimes called "caps" because they go on over the teeth.

Oral Surgery

Dentists sometimes need to *extract*, or pull, a tooth. This might be necessary if a tooth gets broken off or has serious decay.

Dentists who specialize in this kind of work are called *oral surgeons*. Many people visit an oral surgeon to have their wisdom teeth extracted. Wisdom teeth are the last teeth people get—usually, around the age of 20. They often cause problems, so they're extracted.

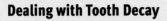

Dealing with Tooth Decay

Tooth decay is a process that gradually creates a small hole, called a *cavity*, in your tooth. A combination of food and bacteria (or germs) causes the decay. The bacteria in your mouth feed on sugars in the food you eat. Then the bacteria produce acids that eat away at your teeth. When a cavity forms, your tooth will probably ache.

How can you prevent tooth decay?

- Brush your teeth (all surfaces) and tongue (back to front) at least twice a day.
- Use toothpaste that contains fluoride.
- Limit your sweet snacks and drinks.
- Eat foods containing calcium, such as dairy products.
- Floss your teeth once a day.
- Replace your toothbrush every three months.
- Rinse daily with a mouth-wash that kills bacteria.

Orthodontic Services

Straight, evenly spaced teeth create a great smile. They also help a person bite and chew correctly.

An *orthodontist* is a dentist who specializes in straightening crooked teeth. A lot of children and teens visit an orthodontist to have braces put on.

Cosmetic Treatments

Some dental treatments are done for the purpose of improving appearance. For instance, bleaching teeth, or "whitening," has become a popular cosmetic service. Dentists may also use porcelain to hide dental flaws and to improve someone's bite or smile.

Pain Control

Modern dental treatments are usually pain free, thanks to skilled dentists and the use of local anesthetics such as Novocain. A *local anesthetic* is a drug that makes a specific area numb and thus pain free.

Dental work that's likely to be uncomfortable may be done under a general anesthetic. A *general anesthetic* puts the patient to sleep, making him or her pain free.

Cosmetic
Done to improve appearance or beauty.

[FACT]

Dental Insurance

Many people get dental insurance as a job benefit from their employer. Other people buy their own insurance because of the high cost of dental care. Having dental insurance helps control what you have to pay for dental work. Like health insurance, dental insurance can prevent you from going into debt if you have serious problems.

Basic dental insurance covers these kinds of dental work:

- **Preventive care and diagnostics (testing):** Most policies cover two visits a year for a check-up or exam, cleaning, X-rays, and treatments that prevent decay and gum disease.

- **Basic restorative care:** Many policies cover half or more of the cost of fillings, crowns, extractions, repairing chipped teeth, and sometimes doing root canals.

- **Major dental work:** Some plans cover at least part of the cost of work such as oral surgery and braces.

Should you get dental insurance? To decide, figure out what you spend a year for dental care. Divide that amount by 12 to determine a monthly average. Then find out what dental insurance would cost you each month. Compare the monthly premium to your average cost.

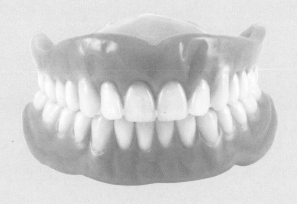

CHAPTER 4

Mental Health

Everyone faces mental stress and strain. And everyone feels sad or confused from time to time.

How do you deal with your unpleasant emotions when life gets tough? How do you relax? Where do you go for help?

Help Yourself

Take a deep breath! People in a hurry or under stress tend to take shallow breaths. So when you feel tense, breathe deeply. Fill your lungs, count to four, and then let out the breath.

Another way to have good mental health is to have good physical health. Keep active and fit. Exercise can melt away stress. At the end of a stressful day, go for a run or shoot some hoops. Also eat well and get plenty of rest. Being well rested can make you feel more able to face life's challenges.

Doing creative activities can relax your mind and lift your spirit, too. Try dancing or singing, painting or drawing for enjoyment and relaxation.

Finally, reach for a "security blanket." Special items can make us feel safe when facing stress and tension. Wearing "lucky" sneakers might calm an athlete's nerves. Carrying a special coin might settle an actor's stage fright. What makes you feel safe and secure?

Confide in Friends

Talk about it! Just putting a problem into words can make you feel less anxious about it.

Confide
To share personal information or secrets.

There are several different ways to talk about your troubles:

→ When stress gets really hard to handle, go to someone you trust. It might be a parent, a favorite teacher, or an older brother or sister.

You might want this person just to listen, or you might want his or her advice and support.

→ If you're uncomfortable talking to someone about your problems, try writing about them in a journal. Organizing your thoughts in writing might help you sort them out and see them more clearly.

[FACT]

Mental Health Insurance

Do you have a group plan for health insurance that covers mental health or substance use disorders? Does the group have at least 50 participants?

If you can answer "Yes" to both of these questions, then you have the same coverage for mental health care as you have for all other medical treatment. This became a US law in 2010, when the Mental Health Parity and Addiction Equity Act (MHPAEA) was passed.

Seek Professional Help

At times, you might need to share your feelings with a professional. A mental health counselor or therapist is trained to help people sort through their problems.

At a ***therapy*** session, a professional may meet with you one on one, with you and your partner or family, or with you and other people facing similar situations. In a *support group*, you'll get a chance to express your emotions. You'll also learn about your strengths and weaknesses. And you'll get help with stopping unwanted behavior and communicating your feelings more clearly.

How can you find a good therapist or counselor? Ask people you trust to recommend someone. You might ask family members, religious leaders, or your family doctor. At school, you can find help by talking to a trusted teacher or guidance counselor. Or you can contact local mental health centers.

Keep in mind that the first therapist you see might not be right for you. If that happens, keep looking! Counselors and therapists have different personalities and different styles. To get the best support and guidance, you'll need to find someone who's a good fit for you.

Therapy

Treatment to heal or cure.

Types of Therapists and Counselors

Professional therapists and counselors have a variety of training and backgrounds, including some type of graduate-level degree. They may be psychologists, social workers, marriage and family therapists, or psychiatrists.

All of these professionals are qualified to provide counseling services. But in most states, only psychiatrists are allowed to prescribe medicines. That's because psychiatrists are trained as medical doctors. If you need medicine and are not seeing a psychiatrist, your counselor will make a referral to a psychiatrist or your regular doctor for a prescription.

Tips for Finding a Therapist or Counselor

Before you make an appointment, interview several therapists or counselors over the phone. Ask these questions:

- What are your professional qualifications, including education, license, or certification?
- How long have you been in practice?
- What area do you specialize in: individuals? families? people who have been abused?
- What are your fees? How are they billed?
- Do you accept my insurance? (Or if you don't have insurance, ask, Do you offer reduced fees or a payment plan?)

At your first appointment, ask these questions to help determine if this is the right therapist or counselor for you:

- How can you help me with my problems?
- What kind of treatment do you use?
- How long will counseling last?

What Is PTSD?

Posttraumatic stress disorder (PTSD) is a condition that can affect anyone who has seen or experienced something horrible and frightening. Some people develop PTSD after one or more of these experiences:

- Military combat
- Sexual or physical abuse or attack
- Terrorist attack
- An accident, such as a car crash
- A natural disaster, such as a fire, earthquake, or tornado

Whether someone develops PTSD depends on factors such as these:

- How serious or long the bad experience was
- Whether the person was hurt or lost a friend or family member in the experience
- How much the person felt in control during the experience
- How much help and counseling the person gets after the experience

Symptoms of PTSD are as follow:

- Replaying the experience in his or her mind
- Avoiding things that bring back memories of the experience
- Feeling numb or being unable to feel emotions
- Watching for or expecting danger in every situation

Handling Health Problems

How sick do you have to be before you go to the doctor? Knowing common signs of illness can help you make that decision. It can also help you know what kind of medicine you may need to get better: one from the drugstore or the doctor. And perhaps most important of all, knowing common signs of illness can help you decide when the situation is an emergency.

Playing "Doctor"

Ronda hadn't felt good for several days. She felt kind of achy and sweaty. She also had a scratchy throat.

"I probably have the flu," she told herself. She'd read online about the start of flu season.

Ronda looked through the medicine cabinet in her family's home. She was sure she could find something that would help her get well. But what? Should she take a pain reliever? An antacid? Throat lozenges?

Ronda decided to take cold and flu medicine. The signs of illness listed on the package matched her own signs pretty closely. The directions said to drink a small cup of the medicine four times a day. So that's what she did.

But the next day, Ronda felt even worse. Her throat was so sore that she could barely swallow. And she felt more achy and hot. She wished she had a thermometer and could take her temperature. She was sure she had a fever.

Ronda called in sick to work. She told her supervisor, Karen, what was wrong. Karen insisted that Ronda go to the doctor. "It sounds like you have a fever," Karen said.

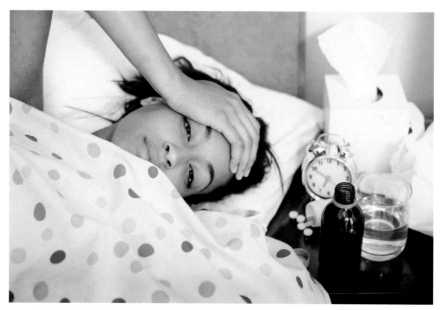

Ronda called her doctor's office and told the nurse how she felt. "Come in right away," the nurse told her. "We're seeing a lot of strep throat right now."

Ronda went in, and the doctor examined her. She had a fever of 102! The doctor also ran a couple of tests, and the results were clear: strep throat.

The doctor gave Ronda a prescription for an antibiotic, which is a bacteria-killing medicine. That's what she needed to get well—not cold and flu medicine. Ronda wished she would have gone to the doctor sooner.

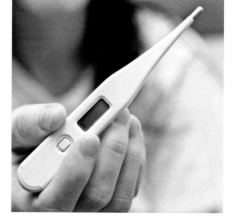

Recognizing Warning Signs

When your car's warning light comes on, it tells you something is wrong. In a similar way, your body uses warning signs such as pain and fever to **signal** trouble.

It's important to pay attention to what your body tells you. To do that, you need to become familiar with the **symptoms** of common health problems. If you notice these symptoms, get help.

General Warning Signs

The following general symptoms indicate that something may be wrong with your body:

→ Aches and pains

→ Fever, especially over 101 degrees Fahrenheit (98.6–99.6 degrees Fahrenheit is normal)

→ Coughing

→ Sneezing

→ Unexplainable weight gain or loss

→ Sores that don't heal

→ A rash

→ Feeling strange or unusual

→ Dizziness

→ Problems sleeping

→ Feeling tired

Don't ignore these symptoms! If they continue, see a doctor.

Common Health Problems

You should also be able to recognize the symptoms of common health problems:

Allergies

→ Frequent and watery runny nose

→ Itchy, watery eyes

→ Symptoms occur during certain seasons

→ Taking antibiotics does not help *relieve* symptoms

Bacterial Infection

→ Fever

→ Cough with rust- or green-colored mucus (the substance that's coughed up)

→ Pain in a specific area

→ Taking antibiotics helps relieve symptoms

Skin Cancer

→ Sores that don't heal

→ Change in the size, color, shape, or border of a mole

→ Appearance of a mole of varied colors, especially red, white, or blue

Signal	Symptoms	Relieve
To indicate or suggest.	Signs of illness or disease.	To reduce or lessen.

→ Continual sadness

→ Trouble sleeping or sleeping too much

→ Frequent and uncontrollable anger

→ Change in appetite

→ Feelings of hopelessness

→ Difficulty completing tasks

→ Lack of enjoyment of friends and activities

[FACT]

Viral versus Bacterial Infections

Do you know the difference between a viral and a bacterial infection? Viruses cause viral infections. Bacteria cause bacterial infections.

Often, the symptoms of the two conditions are the same. But the treatments are different.

Type of Infection	Illnesses Caused	Treatment Needed
Viral	• Cold or runny nose • Flu • Most coughs and bronchitis (chest cold) • Most sore throats • Chicken pox • AIDS (acquired immune deficiency syndrome) • Hepatitis	• Rest • Drink fluids • Humidify your room by running a vaporizer • Avoid smoke and pollution • Take a painkiller or decongestant • See a doctor to treat a serious condition
Bacterial	• Strep throat • Urinary tract infections • Skin infections • Tuberculosis	• Antibiotics—see a doctor
Can be either viral or bacterial	• Pneumonia • Ear infections • Sinus infections • Meningitis • Diarrhea	• See a doctor to find out what you have and how to treat it

Walk-In Clinics

So-called walk-in clinics are located in some national chain stores, such as Target and Wal-Mart. These clinics were created with the goal of providing convenient and affordable health care. Many of the people who go to walk-in clinics don't have regular doctors. These people might not get health care if walk-in clinics weren't available.

So, what's good and bad about walk-in clinics? What are the pros and cons?

Pros

- You don't need an appointment but can make one, if you want to.
- Visits are quick—usually less than 15 minutes.
- The clinics have convenient locations and hours.
- The prices for different services are clear.
- Lower prices than at an urgent-care center or emergency room.
- You can pay with cash or through your insurance.
- Electronic health records are kept.

Cons

- A short visit may not allow enough time for a thorough exam.
- A medical doctor isn't usually on site. Care is provided by nurse practitioners and nurses at most clinics.
- These clinics can't treat every kind of medical problem.
- No follow-up care is provided for long-term conditions or serious problems.
- The quality of care varies from clinic to clinic and state to state.
- Going to this type of clinic may prevent you from building a relationship with a primary care physician.

[FACT]

What You Should Know about Allergies

Common Allergies

- Pollen (produced by plants)
- Dust mites
- Mold
- Latex rubber
- Animal dander (from hair and fur)
- Certain foods
- Bee and other insect stings

Possible Symptoms

- **Mild:** Rash or hives. Itchy, watery eyes. Mild congestion (stuffed-up nose and sinuses). Affects one area of the body.
- **Moderate:** Difficulty breathing (asthma). Itching, hives, or swelling that spreads.
- **Severe (anaphylaxis):** Sudden, life threatening. Affects whole body. Worsens quickly. Can include throat swelling, extreme difficulty breathing, stomach pain, cramps, vomiting, diarrhea, hives, dizziness, and confusion.

Treatment

- Avoid the allergen (the cause of the allergy).
- Take an oral medicine (through the mouth) to stop the itching, swelling, and congestion.
- Use an oral or inhaled (breathed-in) medicine to ease breathing difficulty.
- Get allergy shots (for asthma or allergies to pollen or bee stings).
- Get a shot of epinephrine for a bee sting (for people who have an extreme, life-threatening reaction).
- Call 9-1-1 or go to the emergency room at the first sign of a severe reaction, such as swelling of the throat and difficulty breathing.

[FACT]

Antibiotics: "Wonder Drugs"

Antibiotics are drugs that fight bacterial infections. The first antibiotic was penicillin. It was discovered in the late 1920s and became widely available for use in the 1940s. Penicillin was considered a "wonder drug" because of the number of lives it saved. Before the discovery of this drug, people often died of bacterial infections.

Today, antibiotics are some of the most often prescribed medicines. But taking them incorrectly can do you more harm than good.

Antibiotics work by weakening your immune system. They kill the bacteria in your body. In most cases, you feel better almost immediately after starting to take an antibiotic.

But the effectiveness of antibiotics has two drawbacks:

1. Antibiotics kill the good bacteria in your body along with the bad bacteria. Good bacteria are needed to stay healthy.

2. If you take antibiotics often, the bad bacteria in your body can begin to resist the drugs. When this happens, antibiotics won't work to treat infection anymore.

To avoid having this happen, don't take antibiotics unless you have a bacterial infection.

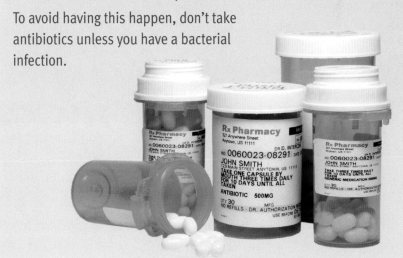

CHAPTER 2

Quick Action: First Aid and the Emergency Room

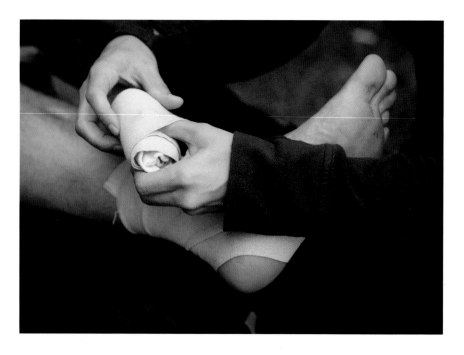

Kim took a first aid class through the American Red Cross. She learned how to treat common injuries, such as insect bites, small cuts, minor muscle strains, and bruises.

Kim also learned how to recognize an emergency and where to get help in emergency situations. Having this knowledge could save a life.

Medical Emergencies

You should call for help when you or someone you're with has any of these injuries or conditions:

→ A large or deep wound or burn

→ A severe facial, head, neck, or back injury

→ Bleeding that won't stop

→ Continuous, nonstop vomiting or diarrhea

→ Sudden, severe, or continuing pain, especially a headache

→ Choking

→ A very high fever

→ Blacking out (losing consciousness)

→ **Extreme** behavior change (such as confusion)

→ Seizures (uncontrolled body movements)

→ Extreme chest pain

→ Evidence of poisoning (even without physical symptoms)

Extreme
Severe or tremendous. To the greatest level or degree.

Basic Supplies for Your Home First-Aid Kit

- Adhesive bandages in various sizes
- Gauze pads in various sizes
- Triangular bandages
- Elastic roller bandages
- Adhesive tape
- Scissors, needle, tweezers
- Antiseptic solution or moist towelettes
- Antibiotic ointment

- Thermometer
- Petroleum jelly or other lubricant
- Hand sanitizer
- Safety pins in various sizes
- Protective gloves
- Cotton balls and cotton-tipped swabs
- Instant cold packs
- First-aid manual

Dialing 9-1-1

If Kim sees someone with any of these signs, she calls to get help from emergency medical services (EMS). In most places, that number is 9-1-1.

When Kim calls, she's ready to give her name and phone number. She's also ready to tell the EMS **dispatcher** the exact location where help is needed: the address, apartment number, closest cross street, and nearby **landmarks**. And she's ready to answer all questions. Kim knows she shouldn't hang up the phone until she's told to and that she needs to follow all instructions.

Going to the Clinic versus the Emergency Room

Sometimes, a medical condition seems **urgent** but not immediately life threatening. In these cases, Kim may take the patient in for treatment herself. For example, a sprained ankle or cut that doesn't spurt blood calls for a visit to a clinic or doctor's office—not the emergency room.

Dispatcher

Someone who answers telephone calls asking for help and sends the needed assistance.

Urgent

Needing immediate attention.

Landmarks

Well-known or commonly seen sites. Examples of landmarks are statues, bridges, and well-known buildings.

If it's after hours at the clinic or the primary care physician isn't available, Kim goes to the hospital emergency room (ER). Going to the ER isn't her first choice, though, for several reasons.

A visit to the ER is the most expensive kind of medical care. Also, getting medical attention can take a very long time. True emergencies are handled first. This means that patients without emergencies may have to wait several hours to be seen. And when they need follow-up care, these patients will have to see other doctors. An ER isn't set up to provide this kind of medical care.

[FACT]

The Facts about 9-1-1

9-1-1

- The 9-1-1 system was set up in 1967. The US government wanted to create a single, nationwide number to make emergency calls to police departments. The Federal Communications Commission (FCC) worked with the nation's largest telephone company to set up that number.

- The first 9-1-1 call in the United States was made in 1968. Gradually, towns and cities across the country set up 9-1-1 service. And over the years, technology updates have improved the speed and handling of 9-1-1 calls.

- Making a 9-1-1 call from a landline telephone will probably get help quicker than making a call from a cell phone. Landline phones are tied to locations, but cell phones are not.

- Calling 9-1-1 as a joke is against the law in most states. But if you call 9-1-1 by mistake, don't hang up. Explain what happened so the dispatcher will know there's no emergency.

Emergency Rooms versus Trauma Centers

Most hospitals have an emergency department, often called the *emergency room (ER)*. It handles emergency illnesses and injuries. Examples include sudden and severe stomach pain, shortness of breath, and severe vomiting or diarrhea. Some of these conditions may be life threatening.

Certain hospitals have *trauma centers*. They provide immediate, life-saving care for people with extreme injuries. Examples include victims of car crashes, gunshot wounds, and earthquakes or tornadoes. To survive, these patients often need immediate treatment by a team of specialists and surgeons. Those kinds of medical professionals are found at trauma centers.

Each state reviews its hospitals to determine which ones have the staff and equipment needed to be trauma centers. States set standards for different levels of care. Level I trauma centers have the highest standard of care.

CHAPTER 3

Prescription Medicines

When Eric had an ear infection, his doctor prescribed an antibiotic to fight it. The doctor filled out a prescription form and gave it to Eric to take to the pharmacy. Eric also had the option of having the doctor's office phone in the prescription. Eric could then stop by the pharmacy later and pick up the medicine.

A prescription form contains the name of the drug being prescribed and the proper *dosage*. It also tells how many times the prescription can be refilled and in what time frame.

Never Share Prescription Medicines

When Eric walked into the pharmacy, he saw his friend Jasper. Eric explained that he'd been to the doctor and showed Jasper the prescription.

"I have some of that medicine at home," said Jasper. "You can have mine and save your money."

"No," Eric answered. "I'll get my own."

Eric had heard that it's not a good idea to share prescription drugs. Sharing medicines can lead to dangerous drug *interactions*, wrong dosages, and allergic reactions, among other things.

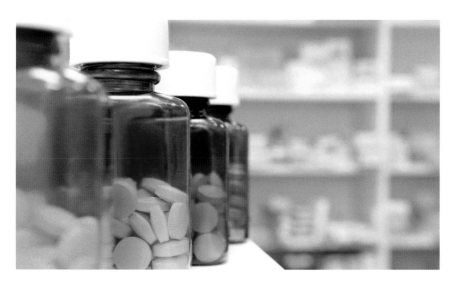

Dosage
The amount or quantity of a drug to take for a single treatment.

Interaction
The effects that occur when two drugs or a drug and another substance are taken together.

Avoid Drug Interactions

Do you take any prescription or over-the-counter drugs? If so, be sure you know how and when to take them. Drugs can mix badly with other medicines and with food, alcohol, and caffeine. Even vitamins and other supplements can interact badly with some drugs.

Here are some examples of bad drug interactions:

- Taking aspirin and blood thinners together can cause extreme bleeding.

- Antibiotics don't work well when taken with antacids or iron supplements.

- Taking an antihistamine will increase the effects of drugs intended to make you calm or sleepy.

Also keep in mind these guidelines concerning medicines and eating:

- Drugs can change your appetite and how your body uses food.

- Mixing medicine into a food or hot drink may stop it from working.

- Taking some drugs with food can cause an upset stomach.

- Some drugs are supposed to be taken after you eat so there's food in your stomach.

Talk to the Pharmacist

Eric's family had always shopped at Fred's Friendly Pharmacy. They had known Fred for years and trusted his professional judgment. Pharmacists aren't doctors, but they know a lot about different kinds of medicines.

"Hi, Eric," Fred said. "Let's see what you've got here today."

Fred looked at Eric's prescription slip and asked, "Will you accept a **generic** brand of this drug?"

Fred explained that a less-familiar brand of drug would be much cheaper than the most well known brand. He

Generic

Common or general. When used to refer to medicine, a *generic* is a drug that does not have a brand name but works the same as a brand-name drug.

assured Eric that the medicine was the same. Eric agreed to accept the generic.

A few minutes later, Fred came back to the counter. Eric's prescription was ready. Since Eric had not used the drug before, Fred explained the dosage instructions and side effects the drug could cause.

"If you become sleepy, dizzy, or have a dry mouth, check with your doctor," Fred warned.

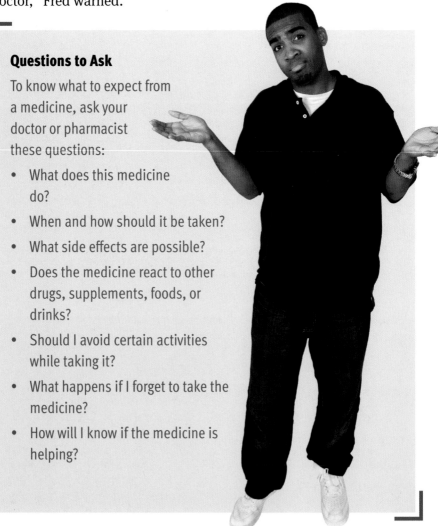

Questions to Ask

To know what to expect from a medicine, ask your doctor or pharmacist these questions:

- What does this medicine do?
- When and how should it be taken?
- What side effects are possible?
- Does the medicine react to other drugs, supplements, foods, or drinks?
- Should I avoid certain activities while taking it?
- What happens if I forget to take the medicine?
- How will I know if the medicine is helping?

SAFER Medicine

When taking any kind of medicine, always think SAFER:

- **S:** Speak up.
- **A:** Ask questions.
- **F:** Find the facts.
- **E:** Evaluate your choices.
- **R:** Read the label for guidance.

Read the Label

Fred also explained the label of the pill bottle to Eric. The label looked like the illustration below.

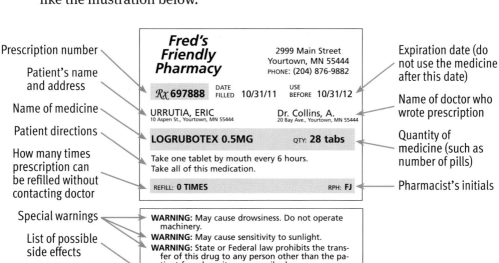

Prescription number

Patient's name and address

Name of medicine

Patient directions

How many times prescription can be refilled without contacting doctor

Special warnings

List of possible side effects

Description of pills to help patient confirm it's the right medicine

Fred's Friendly Pharmacy

2999 Main Street
Yourtown, MN 55444
PHONE: (204) 876-9882

℞ **697888**   DATE FILLED 10/31/11   USE BEFORE 10/31/12

URRUTIA, ERIC
10 Aspen St., Yourtown, MN 55444

Dr. Collins, A.
20 Bay Ave., Yourtown, MN 55444

LOGRUBOTEX 0.5MG   QTY: **28 tabs**

Take one tablet by mouth every 6 hours.
Take all of this medication.

REFILL: **0 TIMES**   RPH: **FJ**

WARNING: May cause drowsiness. Do not operate machinery.
WARNING: May cause sensitivity to sunlight.
WARNING: State or Federal law prohibits the transfer of this drug to any person other than the patient for whom it was prescribed.
Rx: Please read enclosed patient information.
NOTE: This medicine is a white, round tablet imprinted with Logrubotex 0.5.

Expiration date (do not use the medicine after this date)

Name of doctor who wrote prescription

Quantity of medicine (such as number of pills)

Pharmacist's initials

CHAPTER 4

Over-the-Counter Medicines

You can find hundreds of over-the-counter (OTC) medicines on the shelves of your local supermarket, discount store, or drugstore. These products compete for your attention and your dollar. Choosing one can be difficult. Whenever you have questions, talk to your doctor or pharmacist.

Common Over-the-Counter Medicines

The following chart lists some of the OTC products you may have at home in your medicine cabinet:

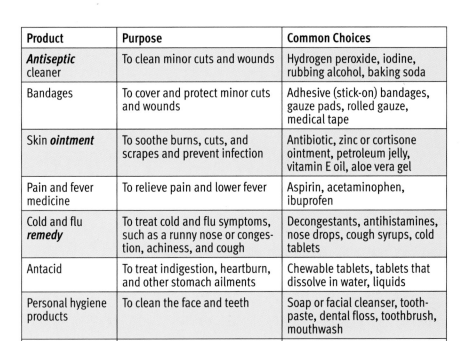

Product	Purpose	Common Choices
Antiseptic cleaner	To clean minor cuts and wounds	Hydrogen peroxide, iodine, rubbing alcohol, baking soda
Bandages	To cover and protect minor cuts and wounds	Adhesive (stick-on) bandages, gauze pads, rolled gauze, medical tape
Skin *ointment*	To soothe burns, cuts, and scrapes and prevent infection	Antibiotic, zinc or cortisone ointment, petroleum jelly, vitamin E oil, aloe vera gel
Pain and fever medicine	To relieve pain and lower fever	Aspirin, acetaminophen, ibuprofen
Cold and flu *remedy*	To treat cold and flu symptoms, such as a runny nose or congestion, achiness, and cough	Decongestants, antihistamines, nose drops, cough syrups, cold tablets
Antacid	To treat indigestion, heartburn, and other stomach ailments	Chewable tablets, tablets that dissolve in water, liquids
Personal hygiene products	To clean the face and teeth	Soap or facial cleanser, toothpaste, dental floss, toothbrush, mouthwash
Sunscreens	To prevent sunburn	Lotions, creams, sprays

Antiseptic

Controlling infection.

Ointment

A gel or cream.

Remedy

A treatment or medicine.

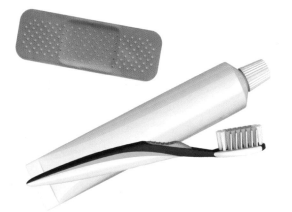

Curing the Common Cold

Many people have a favorite cold remedy. But what remedies do and don't work?

What Works

- Drinking lots of clear fluids
- Gargling with saltwater (mix ½ teaspoon per 1 cup of warm water)
- Using saline nasal drops and sprays for congestion
- Taking a zinc supplement (but not a nasal spray)
- Eating chicken soup
- Taking cough and cold medicines (but not for young children)
- Using antihistamines (but the side effects are heavy)
- Increasing humidity with a room vaporizer

What Doesn't Work

- Drinking alcohol or caffeine
- Taking antibiotics
- For children under age 2, using cough and cold medicines

What Might Help

- Taking vitamin C (especially before you get a cold)
- Taking echinacea

[FACT]

Which Sunscreen Should You Buy?

In 2011, the US Food and Drug Administration (FDA) put out new rules for sunscreen labels. The rules were designed to make it easier for people to know which sunscreen offers the best protection. In particular, people are advised to choose sunscreens that provide protection from skin cancer.

Look for these terms in choosing a sunscreen:

- Products labeled *broad spectrum* provide protection from both ultraviolet A (UVA) and ultraviolet B (UVB) rays. UVA rays age the skin and cause skin cancer. UVB rays burn the skin.

- *SPF* means "sun protection factor." The SPF number is a rating of how well a sunscreen blocks UVB rays. The higher the number (up to 50), the greater the protection from burning.

- Products labeled *water resistant* must say how long they are effective when someone is swimming or sweating: 40 or 80 minutes. Products can no longer claim to be *waterproof* or *sweatproof*.

Guidelines for Buying, Storing, and Using Over-the-Counter Medicines

→ Always read products' labels. If you don't know which product to buy, talk to your doctor or pharmacist.

→ Don't **assume** that a drug is safe just because it doesn't require a prescription.

Assume

To believe or accept without having proof. To take for granted.

→ Follow directions for OTC medicines carefully. Avoid taking too little or too much.

→ Many different brands are available of most OTC medicines. An expensive, well-advertised product is not necessarily better than a less costly, generic product. As always, when in doubt, ask your doctor or pharmacist for advice.

→ All medicines can cause side effects, such as drowsiness. And many medicines have bad interactions with foods and alcohol. Read the label carefully so you know what to expect.

[FACT]

Treatment for a Poisoned Child

For many years, parents of small children were told to keep something called *ipecac syrup* in the medicine cabinet. Drinking this liquid makes someone vomit. Using it was believed to be an effective way to treat the poisoning of a young child.

But today, parents are advised not to use ipecac syrup. Instead, they should call the poison center if they believe a child has been poisoned. Calling the center will provide expert medical help. If treatment is needed, the parents will be told exactly what to do. And later, the poison center will make a follow-up call to make sure everything is all right.

Parents, child care workers, and others who spend time with young children should keep the number of the poison center posted next to the phone: 1-800-222-1222.

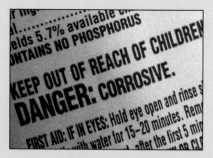

[FACT]

Can You Use Expired Medicines?

Every medicine, whether prescription or over-the-counter, has an expiration date stamped on it. The medicine is supposed to be 100% effective until that date. Marking medicines with expiration dates became a US law in 1979.

But in fact, many medicines are still completely effective long past the expiration date. A study by the US Food and Drug Administration (FDA) found that 90% of drugs were perfectly good 15 years after the expiration date.

Medical professionals agree that taking an expired medicine won't hurt you. But they warn that an old medicine may not be as effective as it's supposed to be. Liquid medicines may lose their effectiveness sooner than dry ones. If a liquid becomes cloudy or changes color, throw it away.

Caution: A few drugs should not be used past their expiration dates: nitroglycerin, insulin, epinephrine, and liquid antibiotics. They cannot be counted on to work.

→ Pay attention to all warnings. Not all medicines are safe for everyone. Conditions such as pregnancy or having a heart ailment may make some drugs dangerous.

→ Check the expiration date on the products in your medicine cabinet. Medicines may be less effective when taken past their expiration date. As a general rule, replace medicines at least every three years.

→ Keep all medicines out of children's reach. No bottle is totally childproof!

Avoiding Health Hazards

Being with your friends can be a lot of fun. But it can also involve making tough choices about your values and behavior. Many young people feel pressure from their friends to use tobacco, drugs, and alcohol. These and other high-risk behaviors can have serious effects on your health and safety. Learn about how these behaviors can affect you and how you can make the choices that are right for you.

The Hardest Thing about College

Ben could hardly believe the first semester was already over. It seemed like just yesterday that he was starting courses at the university.

He thought back to last summer, when he went to freshman orientation. The purpose of orientation was to tell new students about college life. Counselors had talked about choosing a program or major. Students had talked about joining clubs and taking part in campus activities. And professors had talked about how hard the courses would be.

Ben's courses were definitely as hard as the professors had promised. But doing the course work wasn't the hardest thing about college in Ben's view. The hardest thing was dealing with peer pressure.

Peer pressure wasn't anything new to Ben. He remembered middle school and high school. He and his buddies had done some really dumb things—daring each other and showing off for girls. They'd been scolded a couple of times by their parents and teachers. But they'd never gotten into any real trouble.

In college, the stakes were a lot higher. Now, there was pressure to do things like take drugs and drink alcohol. These risky behaviors sometimes had life-changing consequences.

Ben's roommate, Teddy, had been arrested for driving under the influence of alcohol (DUI). He'd gotten drunk at a party and then crashed his car. No one had been hurt, but Teddy was in serious legal trouble. He might also have to drop out of school and work full time to help pay for his legal fees.

Ben had been invited to the same party but decided not to go. He and some friends had gone to a basketball game instead. Ben wondered, though, what would have happened if he'd been with Teddy.

CHAPTER **1**

Resisting Peer Pressure

It's great to have friends! Friends can have fun together. They can also give each other support and advice.

But sometimes, friends can be bad ***influences*** on each other. People of all ages can be influenced by their friends' actions and beliefs. That influence is called ***peer*** *pressure*.

Influence	Peer
To have an effect on. To have control or power over.	A person of your same age or status.

Positive Peer Pressure

Peer pressure can be positive in some situations. For example, Cisco's high school friends are signing up for after-school activities. One is joining a singing group. Another is going out for the volleyball team. Cisco doesn't want to be left out! He follows his friends' lead and decides to join the track team.

Peer pressure has had a positive influence on Cisco. His friends' decisions made him consider doing something new.

Negative Peer Pressure

There's also a negative kind of peer pressure. Take the case of Sophie. A lot of her friends are getting tattoos. Actually, she thinks that body art is ugly. She's also afraid of the health risks and worries how the markings will look 20 years from now. And her parents are completely against the idea of her getting a tattoo!

Still, Sophie wants to fit in with her friends. Should she listen to her own feelings? Or should she do something that may have a negative effect on her health, her body image, and her relationship with her parents?

In some situations, peer pressure can actually be dangerous. And in these situations, making good decisions can be really hard but also really important.

Deana's friend Rosa drives too fast and shows off when she's behind the wheel. Some of their friends think it's funny—but Deana knows better. Should Deana give in to peer pressure and get in the car with Rosa? Or should she be ***assertive***, follow her own good judgment, and stay safe?

Assertive
Confident and strong.

[FACT]

Risk Factors for Teen Drivers

Teens make up only 7% of all drivers, but they're involved in 14% of all car accident deaths. Why is this age group at such high risk for accidents?

- Don't often recognize hazards
- Bad at identifying risks
- Eager to take risks
- Don't always use seatbelts
- Have little driving skill and experience
- Tend to use alcohol and drugs
- Often have passengers
- Have little experience driving at night

Guidelines for Tattoos and Piercings

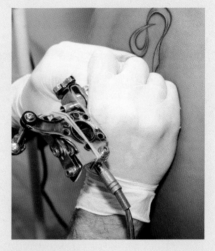

- **Beware of the health risks.** The main risk is getting an infection. Other risks include scarring and having an allergic reaction.

- **Reduce the risks.** Make sure the shop is licensed and has a good reputation. Also make sure the shop is clean. Ask these questions about how things are done:

  —Are needles packaged for one-time use?

  —Is equipment that's reused sterilized after each use to make it germ free?

  —Do the artists wear gloves?

  —Do the artists clean their workstations between clients?

  —Will the artists answer your questions freely?

- **Follow up with proper after care.** Follow all the instructions you're given to ensure proper healing.

Resisting Peer Pressure

Saying "no" to your peers is certainly not easy. It may mean losing a friend, getting laughed at, or being left out of plans and activities. But the more often you stand up for your own values and beliefs, the easier it will get.

When you find yourself being influenced by peer pressure, ask yourself these questions:

1. Am I risking my safety or health?

2. Could this hurt me or someone else?

3. Is this something I really want to do?

4. Will I lose my parents' trust?

Also keep in mind these guidelines for resisting peer pressure:

→ Think in advance about what might be involved in a situation.

→ Avoid activities that involve things you don't want to do.

→ Make decisions that fit your values, not other people's values.

→ Choose friends who influence you in good ways, not bad ways.

→ Practice ways to say "no." Tell the truth or make up an excuse for not getting involved in something.

Learn to think for yourself. Even though "everyone" may be doing it, if something feels wrong, it probably is.

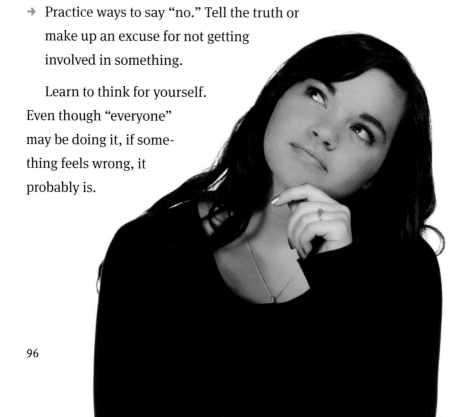

[FACT]

Making Tough Choices about Alcohol, Tobacco, and Drugs

Some of the strongest peer pressure teenagers face involves the use of alcohol, tobacco, and drugs. Consider these facts:

- 72% of teens have drunk alcohol by the end of high school.
- Teens who drink alcohol are 50 times more likely to use cocaine than those who don't drink.
- Alcohol kills 6½ times more teens than all other illegal drugs combined. Most of these deaths are from car crashes.
- 44% of teens have tried cigarettes by twelfth grade.
- 20% of eight-graders have tried marijuana.
- More than 60% of teens say drugs are sold, used, or kept at their school.

CHAPTER **2**

Tobacco

It's a well-known fact that the ***nicotine*** in cigarettes, chewing tobacco, and other tobacco products is dangerous. ***Addiction*** to nicotine can damage health and destroy lives.

Nicotine

The addictive substance in tobacco. Nicotine is a stimulant, which means it excites or speeds up the body's central nervous system.

Addiction

Dependence on a substance. Someone with an addiction has a strong need or craving to use the substance.

[FACT]

What Is Addiction?

Being addicted to a substance like nicotine doesn't mean just wanting or liking to use it. Addiction affects how the brain works and, over time, how much of the body works, too.

Nicotine and other drugs act like chemical messengers called *neurotransmitters* in the brain. Gradually, the brain depends on nicotine to send messages within it and to other parts of the body. These messages control physical functions such as breathing, heart rate, and muscle movement. The messages also affect learning and memory.

Nicotine and other drugs cause the brain to become flooded with a certain neurotransmitter called *dopamine*. Dopamine is sometimes called the "feel good chemical." Having an unusually high level of it in the brain creates a "high" feeling of excitement and pleasure. The brain tries to correct the flood of dopamine by producing less of it. The result is that more and more of the drug is needed to feel the same "high."

When someone stops taking a substance to which the body has become addicted, the body doesn't know what to do. The body responds by going into what's called *withdrawal*. For nicotine, symptoms of withdrawal are restlessness, hunger, depression, and headaches.

99

Serious Health Problems

Studies show that one in every five Americans will die from a disease caused by tobacco use. Common diseases and health conditions from smoking and chewing tobacco include the following:

→ Cancer

→ Stroke

→ Heart disease

→ Circulatory disease

→ Lung disease

→ Osteoporosis (loss of bone density)

→ Damage to unborn babies (caused by tobacco use during pregnancy)

People who use tobacco also have other health issues. Compared to nonsmokers, smokers usually have these issues:

→ Less energy

→ Less *endurance*

→ More coughs and colds

→ Damaged senses of smell and taste

Endurance

The ability to last when faced with a challenge. Sometimes called "staying power."

Dangers of Tobacco Use

- Nicotine is as addictive as heroin and cocaine.
- People who start smoking before age 21 have the hardest time quitting.
- Fewer than 1 out of 10 people who try to stop smoking are actually able to quit.
- After cigarette smoke is inhaled, it takes only eight seconds for nicotine to reach the brain.
- Pure nicotine is so deadly that one drop placed on the tongue will kill someone.
- Addiction to tobacco causes more illnesses and deaths than all other drug addictions combined.
- 80% to 90% of all smokers started as teenagers.
- 70% of smokers under age 18 wish they had never started.

Quitting Tobacco Use

Nicotine is highly addictive, so quitting tobacco use takes hard work and willpower. But people who quit report many health benefits. They also save a lot of money. Tobacco products are expensive!

It seems that many people are making the decision to quit. Studies show that the number of smokers is going down. Nearly 80% of all smokers say they'd like to quit, and about 65% have made one or more serious attempts to quit.

But in one group, the number of cigarette smokers is on the rise. In communities around the world, more teenage girls are starting to smoke. According to the Global Youth Tobacco Survey, 7% of girls between the ages of 13 and 15 smoke cigarettes, and another 8% use

[FACT]

How to Stop Using Tobacco

Most people need help to stop using tobacco products. The most successful way to stop combines medicine with behavioral therapy.

- **Over-the-counter medicines:** Nicotine patches or gums, inhalers, and lozenges can help relieve withdrawal symptoms.

- **Prescription medicines:** Taking a drug such as Zyban or Chantix can help people quit.

- **Behavioral therapy:** Therapy helps tobacco users see their patterns of nicotine use and how to change them. Information may come from self-help materials, telephone "quit lines," or individual counseling.

If you or someone you know is thinking about quitting tobacco use, check out these places that offer help:

- 1-800-QUIT-NOW
  (1-800-784-8669)

- http://www.smokefree.gov

other tobacco products. Another upsetting fact is that 19% of the girls who don't smoke say they feel pressure to start.

Some girls are quitting, too. Carrie was a teen smoker who can now say "I quit!" She writes:

> Smoking was my habit and hobby. Giving up smoking was like losing a friend. I needed to replace it. When I wanted to smoke, I did something else. I took a walk, went to the library, cleaned out a closet. Soon I was enjoying things I'd had trouble with before. I could run farther. I appreciated the smell of my own clean hair. Most of all, I felt powerful. I had taken control. I had beaten the habit.

Quiz about Tobacco Use

If you're a tobacco user or thinking about becoming one, ask yourself these questions:

Yes No

☐ ☐ 1. Does using tobacco make me smarter?

☐ ☐ 2. Does using tobacco make me stronger?

☐ ☐ 3. Does using tobacco improve my appearance?

☐ ☐ 4. Will my family be proud of my decision to use tobacco?

☐ ☐ 5. Will using tobacco get me better grades or a better job?

☐ ☐ 6. Will using tobacco solve my problems?

☐ ☐ 7. Does tobacco taste or smell good?

☐ ☐ 8. Can I come up with one good reason to use tobacco?

CHAPTER 3

Alcohol and Illegal Drugs

Teddy thought it was cool to drink alcohol. And he thought experimenting with illegal drugs was wild and exciting. Life was just one big party in Teddy's view.

Then Teddy discovered the ugly side of using alcohol and drugs. He got behind the wheel of a car after drinking. Using alcohol made him use bad judgment. It made him drive too fast and slowed his *reflexes*.

Teddy crashed his car. Thankfully, no one was hurt. But Teddy knew that he or someone else might have been hurt or even killed.

Teddy was arrested for driving under the influence

Reflexes

Physical reactions or responses. Reflexes occur automatically, without thought or planning.

(DUI). His **BAC (blood alcohol concentration)** was 0.14%—well over the legal limit of 0.08%. In court, a judge **suspended** Teddy's driver's license and sent him to a drug abuse program.

Teddy says going to the program saved his life. It forced him to face the facts about alcohol and drug use.

Getting Help

Help is available for Teddy and others who have problems with alcohol or drug abuse. School counselors, doctors, and social service workers can be helpful sources of information.

Information is also available in the Yellow Pages under "Alcoholism Information and Treatment" and "Drug Abuse Information and Treatment." You can also call the Treatment Referral Helpline

BAC (Blood Alcohol Concentration)

The amount of alcohol in someone's bloodstream, indicated in percent. This may also be called *BAL (blood alcohol level)*.

Suspended

Taken away for a certain time period. In the case of a DUI, a driver's license is usually suspended for up to two years. Suspension is different from *revocation*, which involves a longer or permanent loss of a driver's license.

at 1-800-662-HELP. Counselors will help you find local places for treatment and support groups.

Or go online and find information about treatment at Web sites such as these:

→ **www.findtreatment .samhsa.gov**: Provides referrals to local treatment centers.

→ **http://teens.drugabuse.gov**: Has all kinds of information, including treatment for drugs, alcohol, and nicotine addiction.

Underage Drinking and Driving

In many states, the penalties for getting a DUI are harsher for drivers under 18 than for older drivers. For example, teen drivers often have their licenses automatically suspended for a year. They also face other penalties, such as fines and community service. Several states have also increased DUI penalties for drivers ages 18 to 21. These states want to enforce a zero-tolerance policy for underage drinking. (The legal drinking age is 21 in all states.) Penalties may include a license suspension and even the sale of the vehicle involved in the DUI.

Facts about Alcohol Use

→ Alcohol can kill. Alcohol **overdose** is the number-one drug-related condition seen in hospital emergency rooms. It's also the number-one cause of car accidents.

→ Alcohol can harm health. It can interfere with healthy eating and nutrition. It can cause **permanent** damage to the body.

→ Alcohol can ruin lives. The alcohol that a mother drinks during pregnancy can damage her unborn child.

→ Alcohol can cause legal trouble. In every US state, it's illegal to drink alcohol if you're under 21. It's also illegal to drive a vehicle with a BAC of 0.08% or higher.

Overdose
A dangerous amount of a drug. Taking an overdose can have serious health effects, including stopping breathing, having an irregular heartbeat, and even dying.

Permanent
Lasting or unchanging.

→ Alcohol can lead to addiction. *Alcoholism* is a disease that can strike at any age. Warning signs include drinking to deal with unhappiness, drinking alone or early in the day, missing school or work because of alcohol, needing a drink to "have fun" or "feel at ease," and drinking after deciding to give it up.

Facts about Drug Use

Using illegal drugs may produce feelings of happiness and excitement in the short term. But in the long term, drug use can have serious consequences:

→ Addiction

→ Money problems

→ Legal problems

→ Emotional problems

→ Family and relationship problems

→ Work and school problems

→ Illness

→ Permanent health damage or death

[FACT]

Effects and Risks of Drug Use

Type of Drug	Pleasurable Effects	Health Risks
Depressants: Painkillers and drugs that slow down brain activity	• Feeling less pain • Feeling less anxious or nervous • Feeling happy	• Slow breathing and pulse • Confusion and tiredness • Poor concentration, memory, and judgment • Unconsciousness, coma, and death • Addiction
Stimulants: Drugs that increase activity and effectiveness	• Feeling thrilled • Having more energy • Being more alert or focused	• Heart problems • Restlessness and inability to sleep • Panic attacks • Angry and violent behavior • Addiction
Inhalants: Everyday products with a strong smell	• A brief happy or thrilled feeling	• Stopped heart (and death) • Suffocation (and death) • Seizures • Damage to the liver and kidneys • Permanent brain damage
Marijuana: Dried leaves and flowers of the hemp plant	• Feeling happy or thrilled • Increased senses of sight, hearing, and taste • Feeling relaxed	• Slow reaction time and clumsiness • Poor memory and learning • High blood pressure and heart rate • Panic attacks • Addiction
Anabolic steroids: Artificial form of testosterone (a sex hormone)	• Built-up muscles	• Bones stop growing • Aggressive behavior • Males grow breasts and may become sterile (unable to father children) • Females grow a beard and have a deeper voice

Infectious Diseases

Most of us spend our days with other people. That means we live among germs—both viruses and bacteria. Most germs aren't harmful, but many are **infectious**.

Because germs spread from person to person, we're all likely to catch an illness now and then. Mostly, we come down with short-term

> **Infectious**
>
> Causing infection. *Infectious* diseases can be spread among people through contact.

ailments, like a cold or the flu. But some infectious diseases are serious health threats.

Social Activities with Health Risks

To stay healthy, you need to understand infectious diseases and make efforts not to **contract** any of them. The following sections describe some social activities that may put you at risk for infection. You can stay safe by avoiding high-risk activities or by protecting yourself when you get involved in them.

> **Contract**
>
> To get or catch an illness or disease.

Day-to-Day Contact

→ **Infectious mononucleosis** used to be called "the kissing disease," because it's common among teens and young adults. *Mono*, as this viral infection is called, is usually spread by contact with an infected person's saliva (spit). Early symptoms of mono are lack of energy, a feeling of tiredness, a lack of appetite, and chills. Other symptoms develop within a few days, including a sore throat, fever, and swollen glands in the neck. The main course of treatment for mono is rest.

→ **Strep throat** is a sore throat caused by streptococcal bacteria. Other symptoms include fever and swollen glands in the neck. Strep is most common among school-aged children and teenagers.

However, it's very ***contagious*** and spreads easily among members of the same household. Strep is spread by contact with saliva and droplets spread by sneezing and coughing. Strep throat should be treated with an antibiotic to avoid ***complications***.

Contagious
Able to be spread or shared by contact.

Complications
Medical problems. The term *complications* is often used to mean unexpected problems that occur.

Piercing and Tattooing

Certain risks come with the use of needles. Dirty needles and poor after care can both cause infections and several diseases, as well:

→ **Skin infections:** Getting a tattoo or piercing can lead to a bacterial infection. Symptoms include redness, swelling, pain, and drainage of pus (a thick, yellowish substance caused by infection). Treatment will require use of an antibiotic.

→ **Bloodborne diseases:** Needles and equipment can be ***contaminated*** with infected blood from previous customers. So-called bloodborne diseases can be passed this way, including hepatitis B (HBV), hepatitis C

Contaminated

Made dirty or impure by contact or exposure.

(HCV), and HIV (human immunodeficiency virus), which causes AIDS. Symptoms of hepatitis are like the flu: feeling tired and achy, not having an appetite, and vomiting or having an upset stomach. Hepatitis causes damage to the liver. Treatment with antiviral drugs may be needed. (HIV is discussed in the following section.)

→ **HIV** is contracted by coming into contact with the body fluids of an infected person. HIV can be spread by contact with blood or through sexual intercourse. It is not spread by limited physical contact, such as hugging or kissing or being near someone with the virus. HIV attacks the body's immune system, making it hard to fight other infections and diseases. When the body can no longer defend  itself, the person contracts AIDS (acquired immune deficiency syndrome). There is no cure for HIV/AIDS, but drugs can be used to manage the virus.

→ **STDs (sexually transmitted diseases)** include both bacterial and viral infections. The body's sexual organs are sensitive to bacteria, so infections can be spread through sexual activities such as inter-course. Examples of bacterial STDs are syphilis, gonorrhea, and chlamydia. They can usually be cured with antibiotics. Examples of viral STDs are herpes and viral hepatitis. They can be treated but not cured. In other words, medicine can relieve symptoms but not completely get rid of the disease.

[FACT]

The Facts about STDs

- Each year, 19 million new cases of STDs are reported. About half of them occur in people ages 15 to 24.
- Half of all sexually active young people get an STD by age 25.
- Sexually active teens have the highest STD rates, and they are the least likely to follow guidelines for safe sex.
- Many STDs don't have obvious symptoms. So without testing, it's impossible to know who has an infection.
- STDs can weaken your immune system. They can also lead to developing cancer and other serious diseases.
- Women are infected more easily than men. Women often have more serious health consequences, including infertility (not being able to get pregnant).
- Many STDs can't be cured, and some are life threatening.

Can Sex Ever Be Safe?

There are only two ways to be sure you won't get an STD or HIV/AIDS:

1. Avoid all sexual contact, including kissing. (Some STDs can be passed by the mouth.)
2. Have a relationship with only one partner who has tested free of STDs and HIV/AIDS.

Word List

ability
abuse
accident
ache
activities
addiction
admit
aerobic
alcohol
allergy
antibiotic
anxious
appearance
appetite
application
appointment
approximately
assume
available
average

behavior

cancel
categories
cautious
cavity
check-up
chemical
childproof
college
complain
condition
confide
confident

confuse
consequences
contact
contagious
contain
convenient
counselor
creative
crooked
cure

damage
dangerous
debt
decay
degree
demands
dental
depression
diagnosis
diet
difficult
directions
disease
dosage
drawbacks

eager
effective
embarrassing
emergency
emotional
employer
energy
estimate

evaluate
examine
excitement
expensive
experiences
extreme

factor
fever
flexibility
follow-up
frequent
frustrating

generic
germ
guidance

hazard
hygiene

identify
ignore
illness
immune
indicate
infection
infectious
influence
ingredient
insist
instructions
insurance
interaction
issue

judgment

landmark

medical
medication
medicine
moderate

negative
nutrients
nutrition

obvious
overdose
overweight

package
patient
penalty
permanent
persist
personality
pharmacist
pharmacy
physical
physician
pierce
poisonous
policy
portion
positive
prescription
pressure
preventive

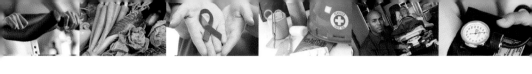

Word List

procedure
process
product
professional
program
provider

qualified
quantity

reaction
recommend
recover
referral
region
regulate
relaxation
release

relieve
remedy
reputable
resist
response
risk
routine

schedule
sensitive
serious
session
severe
shampoo
signal
similar
situation
specialist

specific
status
strain
stress
substance
supplies
support
surgery
symptom

tattoo
temperature
tension
therapist
therapy
thermometer
thorough
threat

tobacco
tough
trauma
treatment

uncomfortable
unexpected
unpleasant
update
urgent
utensils

values
varies
varieties
vocabulary

workout

Index

Index

Index